DATE DUE

SEP 0 1 2008			

30 505 JOSTEN'S

Fact Finders™

Questions and Answers: Physical Science

Sound

A Question and Answer Book

by Fiona Bayrock

Consultant:
Philip W. Hammer, PhD
Vice President, The Franklin Center
The Franklin Institute Science Museum
Philadelphia, Pennsylvania

Capstone press

Mankato, Minnesota

Fact Finders is published by Capstone Press,
151 Good Counsel Drive, P.O. Box 669, Mankato, Minnesota 56002.
www.capstonepress.com

Library of Congress Cataloging-in-Publication Data
Bayrock, Fiona.
    Sound: a question and answer book / by Fiona Bayrock.
    p. cm.—(Fact finders. Questions and answers. Physical science)
    Summary: "Introduces the concepts of sound waves, vibration, and energy, and
presents how humans perceive and produce different sounds"—Provided by publisher.
    Includes bibliographical references and index.
    ISBN-13: 978-0-7368-5449-8 (hardcover)
    ISBN-10: 0-7368-5449-5 (hardcover)
    1. Sound—Juvenile literature. I. Title. II. Series.
QC225.5.B353 2006
534—dc22   2005020128

Editorial Credits
Chris Harbo editor; Juliette Peters, designer; Molly Nei and Tami Collins, illustrators;
    Jo Miller, photo researcher; Scott Thoms, photo editor

Photo Credits
Capstone Press/Karon Dubke, 7, 12, 13, 18, 25, 27, 29 (all)
Comstock Images, cover
Corbis/Bruce Burkhardt, 5; Japack Company, 22; Norbert Schaefer, 15; Tim Pannell, 21
Digital Vision/NASA/Ross Ressmeyer, 11
Getty Images Inc./Visuals Unlimited/Dr. Fred Hossler, 8
Photo Researchers, Inc./Science Photo Library/Sally Bensusen, 10
Stockbyte, 4, 14
UNICORN Stock Photos/A. Gurmankin, 1; Michele Burgess, 17

1 2 3 4 5 6   11 10 09 08 07 06

Table of Contents

Features

What is sound?

Bang, clang, buzz, tap-tap-tap, people talking, music playing, and noise, noise, NOISE. You can't get away from sound. Even when it seems like there is no sound at all, you can still hear something. You might hear your clock ticking or the floor creaking. Sound is everywhere.

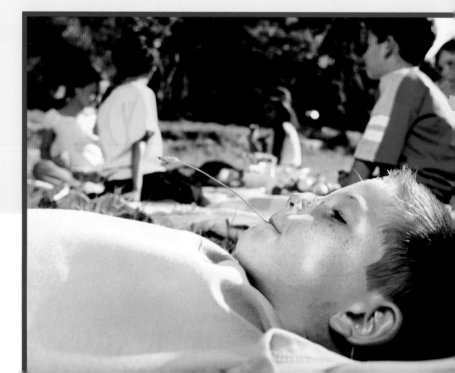

If you take a minute to listen, you might be surprised by all of the sounds you hear.

4

A jackhammer makes a loud racket as it sends vibrations through the air and ground.

So, what is sound? Every sound begins with something **vibrating** back and forth. The vibrations travel to your ears. You can't see sound, but it's there. It's always moving—through the air, the ground, or even walls.

If I could see sound, what would it look like?

When you hit a metal pie plate with a spoon, the plate vibrates back and forth very quickly. Each time it moves, the plate bumps nearby air particles called **molecules**. They bump into the air molecules next to them, which bump into the next ones, and so on.

Fact!

Sound waves and water waves are not the same. Molecules move back and forth in a sound wave. Molecules move in a circular pattern in an ocean wave.

Each tap of the spoon sends sound waves in all directions.

What would the air molecules around the plate look like? You would see waves spreading out as they moved away from the plate. First a wave of air molecules would squish together. Then they would spread apart and squish together over and over again. They would remind you of the ripples a stone makes when it's dropped in a pond.

How do ears work?

The outside of your ear is specially shaped to catch sound waves and direct them into your head. Sound waves move down the ear canal to your **eardrum**. The eardrum is a piece of skin about the size of your smallest fingernail. It vibrates when air molecules give it a push.

Fact!

What are the smallest bones in your body? The ear bones. They are called the hammer, anvil, and stirrup.

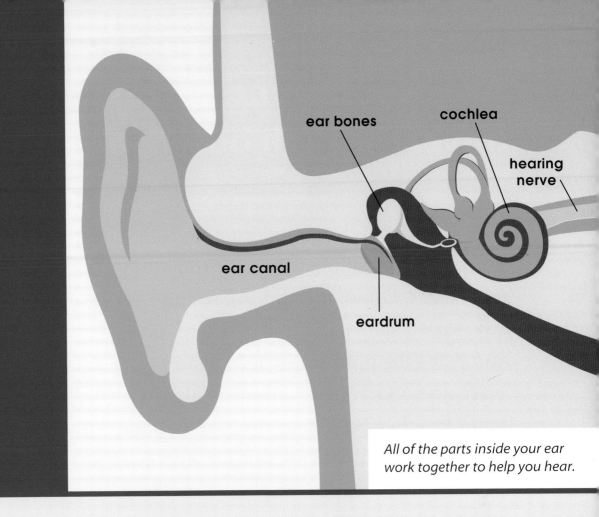

ear bones

cochlea

hearing nerve

ear canal

eardrum

All of the parts inside your ear work together to help you hear.

Once past your eardrum, the vibrations travel through three tiny bones to the **cochlea**. The cochlea is made of fluid-filled tubes all coiled up like a snail shell. It's about the size of a pea. The vibrations travel through the fluid and change into electrical signals. The hearing nerve takes these signals to your brain.

Why can't sound waves travel through outer space?

Sound travels from molecule to molecule. It doesn't matter if the molecules are in a gas, liquid, or solid. All sound waves need something to travel through. And that's the problem in deep space. Space doesn't have enough molecules to bump together. Sound waves have nothing to move through. Making noise in space is like trying to make water waves in an empty bathtub. It doesn't work.

Fact!

The sounds of exploding spaceships you hear in the movies are all fake. In real life, an explosion in space would make no sound at all.

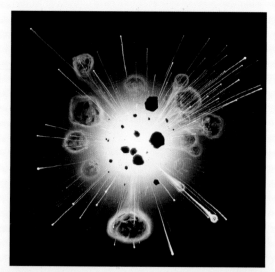

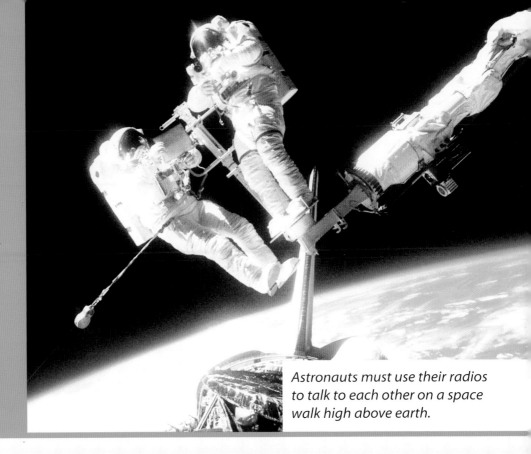

Astronauts must use their radios to talk to each other on a space walk high above earth.

On a space walk, astronauts use radios to talk to each other. Radios turn sound waves into **electromagnetic waves** that can travel through space.

So what if astronauts' radios failed? The sound of their voices can't travel through space, not even an inch. But sound can travel through the molecules in space helmets. Astronauts can touch their helmets together to hear one another.

What do sound waves do in my bedroom?

Sound waves do all sorts of amazing things. When your stereo plays, sound waves bump into everything in the room. Walls, mirrors, and other hard, flat surfaces **reflect** sound. The sound waves bounce off and travel in new directions. Blankets, pillows, and other soft, fluffy things **absorb** sound. They stop it from going anywhere else.

Sound waves bounce off the walls but are absorbed by pillows and blankets.

Sound waves can bounce around corners and travel through walls.

Some sound is transmitted through the walls, right into the next room or outside. Sound waves also bend around the edges of things. This bending is called **diffraction**. Someone down the hall can hear your stereo because sound waves diffract around the doorway.

What makes a sound loud or quiet?

Sound waves carry **energy**. Loud sounds carry more energy than softer sounds. Loud sounds vibrate more air molecules.

Sound waves also stretch wider as they travel. So the energy in them gets spread out over a larger space. The farther you move away, the less energy the sound wave has when it reaches your ears. The sound becomes quieter.

Fact!

Dogs howl when they hear sirens, but not because the sounds hurt their ears. Sirens create sound waves that are similar to those of a dog's howl. Dogs use howls to communicate and to guard their territories. So when they hear sirens, they howl back!

Psst . . . listen up! At 20 decibels, you have to be pretty close to hear someone whisper.

Scientists measure sound in **decibels**. Humans hear a huge range of sounds, so decibels work in an unusual way. A sound that is 10 decibels higher than another is about twice as loud. A jet plane taking off at 120 decibels is more than 1,000 times louder than a whisper at 20 decibels.

What's the difference between high pitch and low pitch?

Pitch makes a sound high or low. Pitch depends on the **frequency** of an object's vibration. Higher pitches vibrate faster. They have shorter sound waves. Lower pitches vibrate slower. They have longer sound waves.

A high-pitched sound makes more sound waves than a low-pitched sound.

High-Pitched Sound

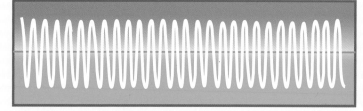

Low-Pitched Sound

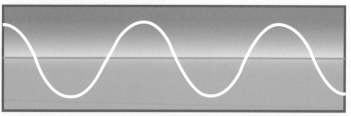

Elephants can talk to each other with rumbling sounds as low as 5 Hz.

Frequency is measured in **hertz** (Hz). One Hz equals one vibration, or sound wave, per second. People can hear sounds between 20 Hz and 20,000 Hz.

But not all ears are equal. Dogs, bats, and dolphins can hear sounds higher than 20,000 Hz. And elephants communicate with each other in sounds lower than 20 Hz.

How fast do sound waves travel?

All sound waves—high or low—travel at the same speed. How is this possible? Think of sound waves as a younger child and an older child walking home together. To arrive at the same time, they walk at the same speed. But the younger child's legs are shorter. She takes more steps to cover the same distance. Sound waves act the same way. High sounds make more waves to reach you at the same time as low sounds.

Short and long sound waves are like short and tall people walking side by side. A shorter person must take more steps to keep up with the stride of a taller person.

How far does sound travel in one second?

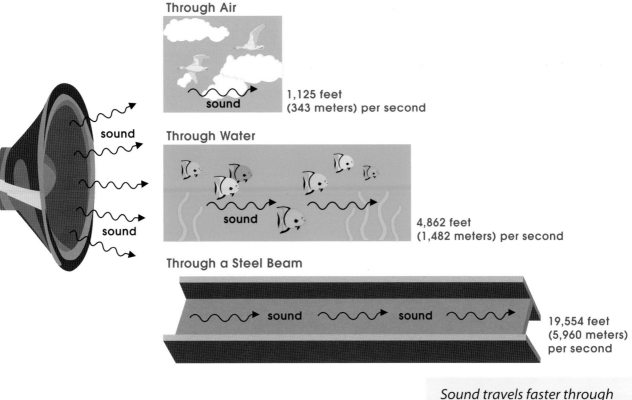

Through Air

1,125 feet
(343 meters) per second

Through Water

4,862 feet
(1,482 meters) per second

Through a Steel Beam

19,554 feet
(5,960 meters)
per second

Sound travels faster through steel because steel's molecules are packed close together.

Exactly how fast sound waves move depends on what they are traveling through. Sound travels faster when molecules are packed tightly together. So sound waves travel faster through water than through air. They move even faster through a solid wall.

Why do my friend and I have different voices?

When you talk, air flows from your lungs past two folds of skin in your throat. These vocal cords vibrate to make your voice. Voice pitch depends on the size of the cords and how stretched they are. Short, thin, tight cords make high sounds. Long, thick, loose vocal cords make deep sounds.

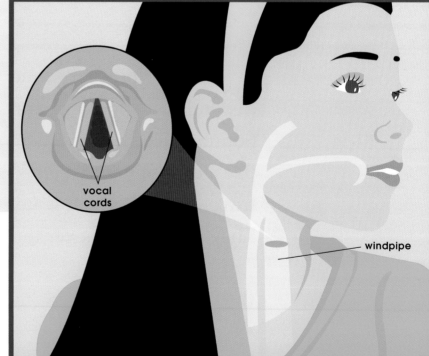

vocal cords

windpipe

The sound of your voice is made by air flowing through your vocal cords.

People have different laughs partly because their vocal cords stretch in different ways.

Throat, tongue, lip, and mouth shapes also affect the way a voice sounds. So does how much sound comes through the nose. Body parts must be exactly the same size and shape for two voices to sound the same. You and your friend have different voices because you're built differently.

What's the difference between noise and music?

Most people agree that an orchestra playing Mozart is music. But while you may think rap is music, your parents are very sure it's noise. And what is "music" in one country may be "noise" to people in another part of the world. Whether sounds make noise or music depends on each person's experience or taste.

A bow vibrates a metal string on a cello to create a note of sound. Many notes together create music.

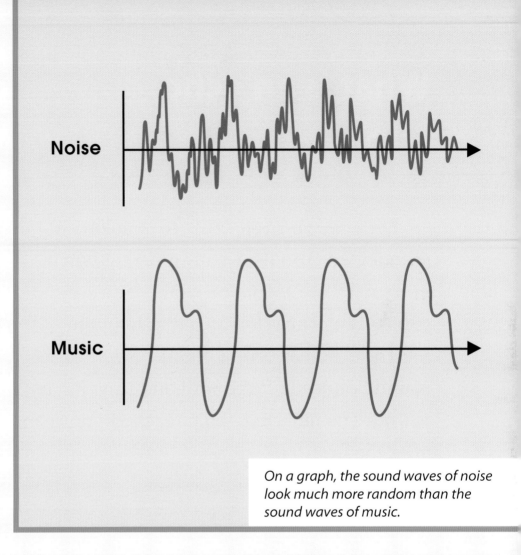

Noise

Music

On a graph, the sound waves of noise look much more random than the sound waves of music.

But look at what people call music. Usually, the sounds of music are organized in some way. Notes made by instruments have sound waves with regular patterns. Graphed sound waves of noise have no pattern. They look jagged and irregular.

What is an echo,
echo, echo?

Let's say you yell "Hi!" to someone in the school gym. You hear your greeting when you say it, but soon after you hear a second "Hi!"— an **echo**! How did that happen?

The echo happened because some of the sound bounced off the wall and traveled back to you. The reflected "Hi!" reached your ears after the first "Hi!"

Fact!

Sound always travels the same speed through the same kinds of molecules. People can measure distance by timing echoes. Scientists use sonar (reflected sound waves) to map the bottom of the ocean or to find submarines and shipwrecks.

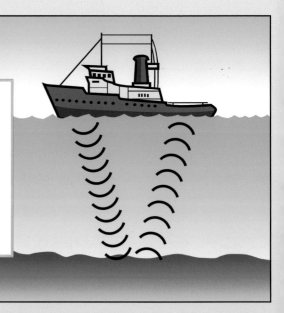

In an empty gym, you hear an echo when your voice bounces off the far wall and back to you.

Sound waves need a lot of energy to make an echo. They must be loud enough to travel to a reflecting surface and then back to your ears. You also need a large reflecting surface. Hard, smooth surfaces work best. Canyons and streets between tall buildings are great places to make an echo.

How can I make music sound better in my bedroom?

Music can sound bad if sound waves bounce back and forth between two walls or the floor and ceiling. Some notes may sound too loud and "pop out."

You can improve your room's **acoustics**, or sound quality. Hang some picture frames on the walls, or put a beanbag chair on the floor. Then sound waves will bounce in many directions instead of just back and forth. Music will sound much better.

Fact!

Wood surfaces absorb low bass sounds. Heavy curtains absorb the high notes. Carpet can help get rid of echoes.

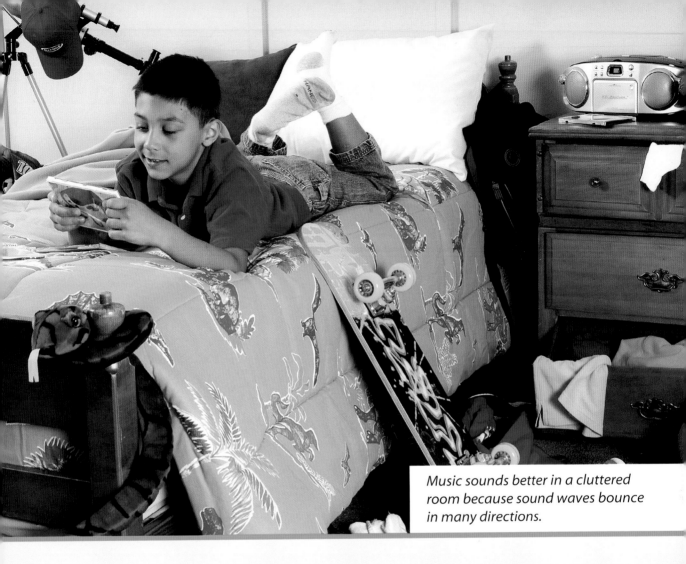

Music sounds better in a cluttered room because sound waves bounce in many directions.

Furniture of different sizes, bookcases, and a coat rack will help. So can putting things on shelves and hanging bulky objects on the walls. And, don't forget to put floor pillows or rugs on the floor, too. Aha! A scientific reason for having a messy room!

Fast Facts about Sound

- All sounds start with something vibrating.

- Sound travels in waves.

- Sound travels faster through water than through air. It travels even faster through a solid.

- Sound waves cannot travel through outer space.

- Sound waves can bounce off, bend around, or go through objects they run into.

- Sound waves carry energy. More energy means louder sound.

- High-pitched sounds are made by shorter, more frequent waves. Low-pitched sounds are made by longer, less frequent waves.

- Humans can hear very deep, low-frequency sounds of 20 Hz to very high-frequency sounds of 20,000 Hz.

Hands On: Sound Waves Travel Where?

See for yourself how sound waves can travel through a solid.

What You Need

Metal coat hanger
2 pieces of string 18 inches
*   (46 centimeters) long each*
table

What You Do

1. *Tie one end of each piece of string to a corner of the coat hanger. Each string should be tied to a different corner.*
2. *Wrap the loose end of one of the strings two or three times around your index finger. Wrap the other string around the end of the index finger on your other hand.*
3. *Hold the strings in place with your thumbs. Lift the strings so the coat hanger swings freely. The hook of the hanger will be pointing down.*
4. *Swing the coat hanger so the hook bumps into the table. What kind of sound did you hear?*
5. *Now place your index fingers gently inside your ears while holding the string pieces. Once again, swing the coat hanger so it bumps the table. Do you hear the sound differently?*

Bumping the coat hanger against the table makes the hanger vibrate. The vibration bumps nearby molecules. The first bump sounded like a click or tap sound. The sound waves traveled through the air to your ear. The second bump, with your fingers in your ears, sounded like a gong or ring. It sounded different because the sound waves traveled through the string and your fingers to get to your ears.

Glossary

absorb (ab-ZORB)—to soak up

acoustics (uh-KOO-stiks)—related to sound or hearing; rooms with good acoustics allow people to hear music clearly.

cochlea (KOH-klee-uh)—a spiral-shaped part of the ear that helps send sound messages to the brain

decibel (DESS-uh-bel)—a unit for measuring the volume of sounds

diffraction (di-FRAK-shuhn)—the bending of sound waves as they pass around the edge of an object

eardrum (IHR-druhm)—a thin piece of skin stretched tight like a drum inside the ear; the eardrum vibrates when sound waves strike it.

echo (EK-oh)—a sound that has bounced back from a distant object

electromagnetic wave (i-lek-troh-mag-NET-ik WAYV)—a wave of electrical and magnetic force created by the vibration of electrons

energy (EN-ur-jee)—the ability to move things or do work

frequency (FREE-kwuhn-see)—the number of sound waves that pass a location in a certain amount of time; a high frequency sound sends more waves past a location in a certain amount of time than a low frequency sound.

hertz (HURTS)—a unit for measuring the frequency of sound wave vibrations; one hertz equals one sound wave per second.

molecule (MOL-uh-kyool)—two or more atoms of the same or different elements that have bonded; a molecule is the smallest part of a compound that can be divided without a chemical change.

pitch (PICH)—the highness or lowness of a sound; low pitches have low frequencies and high pitches have high frequencies.

reflect (ri-FLEKT)—to bounce off an object

vibrating (VIE-bray-ting)—the action of moving back and forth quickly

Internet Sites

FactHound offers a safe, fun way to find Internet sites related to this book. All of the sites on FactHound have been researched by our staff.

Here's how:
1. Visit *www.facthound.com*
2. Type in this special code **0736854495** for age-appropriate sites. Or enter a search word related to this book for a more general search.
3. Click on the **Fetch It** button.

FactHound will fetch the best sites for you!

Read More

Cooper, Christopher. *Sound: From Whisper to Rock Band.* Science Answers. Chicago, Ill.: Heinemann, 2004.

Cooper, Jason. *Sound.* Rourke Discovery Library. Vero Beach, Fla.: Rourke, 2003.

Dreier, David Louis. *Sound.* Science Around Us. Chanhassen, Minn.: Child's World, 2005.

Olien, Rebecca. *Sound.* Our Physical World. Mankato, Minn.: Bridgestone Books, 2003.

Index